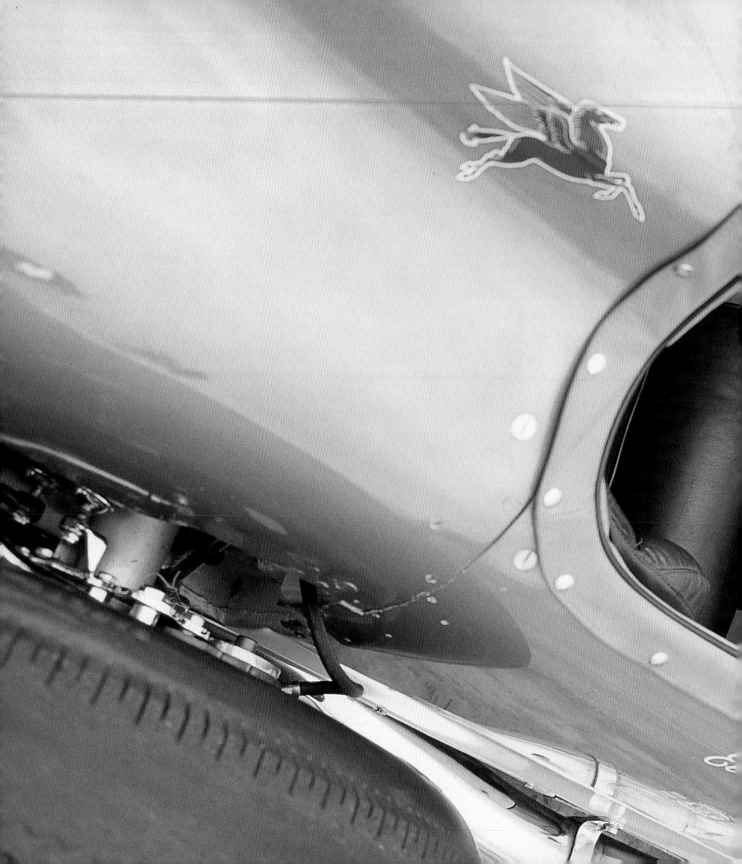

VINTAGE & HISTORIC
INDIANAPOLIS
RACE CARS

Dan Owen

MBI Publishing Company

First published in 1998 by MBI Publishing Company, 729 Prospect Avenue, PO Box 1, Osceola, WI 54020-0001 USA

MBI Publishing Company books are also available at discounts in bulk quantity for industrial or sales-promotional use. For details write to Special Sales Manager at Motorbooks International Wholesalers & Distributors, 729 Prospect Avenue, Osceola, WI 54020-0001 USA.

Library of Congress Cataloging-in-Publication Data

Owen, Dan.
    Vintage & Historic Indianapolis race cars/
    Dan Owen.
        p. cm. -- (Enthusiast color series)
    Includes index.
    ISBN 0-7603-0347-9 (pbk. : alk. paper)
    1. Indy cars. I. Title. II. Series.
    TL236.074   1998
    796.72'09772'52--dc21   98-13186

On the front cover: This was probably the second front-drive car Harry Miller built for the 1925 season. Its outboard-mounted front brakes were the major point of historic contention. All other Miller front-drives had inboard brakes on either side of the transmission. The first front-drive, with inboard brakes, the "Junior Eight" was built for Jimmy Murphy, under General Motors heir Cliff Durant's sponsorship.

On the frontispiece: This wheel belongs on the 1949 Lou Moore "Blue Crown Special." Moore's name and logo appear on the leather headrest and knock-off hubs.

On the title page: With Ernest Ruiz as owner this car first raced at Indy in 1953 with Jim Rathman driving, starting 25th and finishing seventh. The chassis is a Kurtis-Kraft 500B.

On the back cover: This 1968 wedge-shaped Lotus-built chassis shows early effort at making the entire car work as an aerodynamic shape as it moves through the air.

Edited by Anne McKenna
Designed by Katie L. Sonmor

Printed in Hong Kong through World Print, Ltd.

CONTENTS

ACKNOWLEDGMENTS

This book would not have been possible without the help of so many people who gave generously of the cars in their private collections or under their stewardship, as well as their time, information, and their incredible encyclopedic knowledge of the world of vintage racing cars: Craig Agan, Chris Agajanian, Joe Baird, R. J. Buck Boudeman, Chuck Buckman, Dean and Brenda Butler, Chuck Davis, Jim Dilamarter, Junior Dreyer, E. L. Eddie Evans, Dan Fleisher, Joe Freeman, Rick Galles, Ken Gierach, Jim Hoersting, Lou Holland, Lindsey Hopkins III, Parnelli and P. J. Jones, Arlen Kurtis, Jim Lattin, Christopher Leydon, Jim Lockwood, Don Lyons, Dale Lyons, Tom Malloy, Bob McConnell, Don McReynolds, Bill Milliken, Phillip Parnegian, Lynn Paxton, Mitchell Rasansky, Bob Rubin, John Ryals, Norma Salerno, Scott Simpson, Tom Sturm, Robert Sutherland, Bob Swarms, David Uihlein, Judy Vingleman, Martin Walford, Buster Warke, and Ron Watson.

Special thanks to all the "gearheads" on CompuServe Information System's On-Line Motorsports Forum. They are gentlemen and scholars one and all, and contributed so much to this book: Tom Beeler, Dick Carlson, Christopher Etzel, Craig Hibbard, Mike Hollander, and D. M. Woodie Woodhouse.

And last, but certainly not least, to my wife, Pam Owen . . . thanks, babe!

—*Dan Owen*

INTRODUCTION

The Indianapolis Motor Speedway is the oldest continuously operating racetrack besides two New York State Fairgrounds at Syracuse. During its time it has compiled an amazing history.

It has hosted every era of American oval-track racing. It has witnessed heroic and horrible moments in motor racing. It has survived closure during two world wars and neglect during the Great Depression. It has cradled the dreams and decisions of three owners, four sanctioning bodies, and five generations of drivers. It has weathered and surmounted the internal politics of rule changes, engineering progress, the external politics of the "fuel crisis" of the 1970s, and the up-and-down swings of the American economy.

Steeped in tradition, the Indianapolis 500 has become more than just an automobile race; it is part of our history.

Most of the greatest cars in racing, both foreign and domestic, have run at Indy: Marmon, Stutz, Peugot, Frontenac, Duesenberg, Miller, Maserati, Novi, Lotus, and Penske to name just a few.

This book captures a few of the best of these, the cars that changed American racing or milestones that marked automotive progress through the years. It traces the evolution of Indy cars as well as sprint cars and midgets, as each made its contribution to racing and to the cars parked in our own driveways.

Sometimes controversial, many times predictable, since 1909 the Indianapolis Motor Speedway has been the epicenter of American automobile racing. And one simple truth remains: It is "the greatest spectacle in racing."

The comparatively recent and rapidly growing sport of vintage open-wheel racing has done much to fuel interest in these legendary cars and the history that surrounds them. Rolled out of museums, garages, and private collections and onto a paved or dirt oval, these cars are offering new generations of fans a chance to see and hear just a bit of "the way it was."

These are more than merely old race cars; they're milestones in the evolution of the automobile from 1900 to today. They celebrate America's love affair with the automobile and they help us trace automotive development from crude horseless carriages to the computer-controlled sedan. By examining these cars in their restored form we can ascertain the development of racing cars from the early days on America's oval tracks to the current state-of-the-art machines.

Because of the competitive nature of racing, last year's chassis many times becomes discarded when it no longer proves useful. Therefore, very few vintage race cars have survived in their entirety. This book features many of the authentic originals, as well as "bits and pieces" re-creations of the beautiful, historic, vintage Indianapolis race cars.

Cars of this period were suspended high over front and rear axles on straight rail frames with half-elliptic springs controlled by crude friction shocks. This yielded ride heights and roll centers roughly equivalent to a Conastoga wagon. *David Uihlein Collection*

The combination of huge combustion chambers and anemic ignition systems required two spark plugs per cylinder to completely ignite the fuel/air charge. *David Uihlein Collection*

THE EARLY YEARS

1914 MERCER MODEL 45 RACER

From its earliest days the leaders in the automobile industry believed a primary reason for racing was to sell passenger cars. Racing, both on oval tracks and road courses, was seen as advertising—a way to prove the desirability and dependability of the product. Therefore, most early race cars were passenger models—stripped to the essentials of frame, engine, driveline, and suspension—then fitted with a simple "dog house" engine cover and one or two crude seats.

The cars of the Mercer Automobile Company are typical examples. With the introduction of its road-going Type 35 Raceabout in 1911, a serious factory racing program followed. Mercer 35s finished 12th and 15th in the first Indianapolis 500 in 1911. Both cars were driven home afterwards. Mercers of this era were also notable for top finishes at famous road races such as the Elgin National Trophy race in Illinois; the races at Fairmount Park in Philadelphia; and the Savannah, Georgia, Challenge Trophy.

Early wins were scored with these modified stock chassis, but from 1913 onward the company used purpose-built racers designated Type 45 for their team drivers.

A 449-ci displacement limit was instituted for the 1913 season—reduced from the mammoth 1912 formula of 600 cubic inches. The Type 45 had a newly designed four-cylinder racing engine of 445-ci displacement and 150 horsepower. Reliability was always a problem with these long-stroke engines because they tended to pound out their own crankshaft and connecting rod bearings at anything beyond conservative rpm limits.

Mechanical brakes operated on rear wheels only and, combined with the narrow-cross-section tires of the day, made stopping quickly or even slowing abruptly hopeful, if not impossible.

However, the race-winning importance of shorter pit stops was clearly evident even to these early racers. By 1914 most race cars had switched to European-type wire wheels, which slipped over a splined shaft and were secured by a knock-off hub—a marked improvement over bolt-on wooden-spoke wheels with clincher-type rims.

Privately owned Mercers and Mercer-engined "specials" enjoyed continued success over the next few years in both oval and road races. In 1914, during the Elgin National Trophy race, two factory Mercers locked wheels as one tried to pass, resulting in the death of popular factory-driver Spencer Wishart. As a result, the Mercer factory officially withdrew from racing.

This 1914 Mercer Model 45 Racer is a re-creation.

1915 DUESENBERG "WALKING BEAM" FOUR

In an effort to keep European participation in American races at a high level, the 1915 AAA Contest Board lowered engine displacement from 450 cubic inches to 300 cubic inches, in line with the European formula.

The engine in the 1915 Duesenberg was a 299-ci, side-valve, T-head, "walking beam" four. A four-cylinder engine with two spark plugs per cylinder, the walking beam four had two camshafts in the crankcase. The camshafts operated the horizontal overhead valves through long, pivoted rocker arms on the side. Horsepower was approximately 105.

Fred Duesenberg refined and developed this unique valve arrangement. Other manufacturers licensed or "borrowed" the system and walking beam valve operation continued in road automobiles for the next 20 years.

The long, tapering rear section of the Duesenberg shows early aerodynamic efforts that in those days was called streamlining. The boat-tail body was implemented as early as the first Indianapolis race in 1911, on Ray Harroun's race-winning Marmon Wasp, and again in the 1912 Indy on Eddie Hearn's ultra-streamlined Case.

The "Walking Beam" Four had a boat-tail, which was a hollow shell, removable for short track races and remountable for racing on longer or faster tracks. *Joseph Freeman Collection*

The famous Duesenberg "Walking Beam" Four engine design was used in the factory racing team cars in 1915. The chassis features a double-drop frame with kick-ups over both front and rear axles. Cars with this frame style were not built after early 1915. *Joseph Freeman Collection*

From the front wheels to the cowl the car looked conventional. From the cowl back to the tailpipe it resembled a large egg. The body was painted metallic gold and was immediately nicknamed the "Golden Egg." *Michigan Motor Sports Hall of Fame*

The owner of this authentic, original Due-senberg is Joe Freeman who races the car in vintage races today. The car is probably one of five Duesenberg team cars sold in late 1915. The car is a double-drop-frame design with frame kick-ups over both the front and rear axles. The double-drop-frame design was used until early 1915. This Duesenberg has the newer, fancier, 16-valve engine in the older-style, double-drop frame.

Wilbur D'Alene took second place at Indy in 1916 in an identical car. Teammate Ed O'Donnell scored wins on both oval and road courses through the rest of the season.

Unlike their arch-rival Harry Miller, who built only racing cars for anyone who could afford the price, Fred and Augie Duesenberg built and raced a small number of cars in order to promote the reputation and sales of their passenger cars. In the racing world, Miller's cars came to overshadow Duesenbergs in number produced and technology. But the magnificent road-going Duesenberg roadsters, phaetons, and sedans of the 1920s and 1930s are still regarded as some of the most beautiful, powerful, and exciting automobiles of their day.

BARNEY OLDFIELD's **1917** GOLDEN SUB

Every era in American automobile racing has produced its superstars. For a brief moment in history, the unusual Golden Sub brought together two of America's racing giants: Berna Eli (Barney) Oldfield whose star was fading and Harry Artemus Miller whose star was rising. Their stars crossed in 1916.

In the history of American automobile racing, few were more legendary than Barney Oldfield. Hard-driving, hard-drinking, high-living, big-spending, cigar-chomping Barney barnstormed across America bringing the first sight of a racing automobile to rural America. Oldfield spent off-season win-

On August 9, 1917, at a one-mile oval in St. Louis, Missouri, the Golden Egg set new records for 1 mile at 80.0 mph; 5 miles at 77.2 mph; 25 miles at 75.4 mph; and 50 miles at 73.5 mph. *Michigan Motor Sports Hall of Fame*

Bolted to the end of the beautiful, sweeping intake manifold is one of Harry Miller's famous racing carburetors. *Michigan Motor Sports Hall of Fame*

ters in Los Angeles. He knew Harry Miller, who had built a reputation as a builder of successful racing carburetors and, by 1916, had one of the finest automobile machine shops in the West.

The pair made a deal for Miller to design and build an aluminum-bodied car incorporating Miller's new four-cylinder, overhead-cam engine. Ironically, one of the early design parameters called for the car to be completely enclosed for safety reasons. It was a plan that was nearly tragic later.

The engine was the largest, single aluminum casting ever attempted for automotive use at that time. It featured a semi-desmodromic, overhead valvetrain. There were two cams for each rocker arm. One cam pushed the rocker arm down, the other cam pushed the rocker arm back up, but the rocker arm was not attached to the valve. There was a substantial helper-spring on the valve that returned the valve to its closed position.

From the front wheels to the cowl the car looked conventional. From the cowl back to the tailpipe it resembled a large egg. The body was painted a flat gold, hence the name "Golden Sub," but it was immediately nicknamed the "Golden Egg." After an unsuccessful debut the nickname changed to "Golden Lemon."

Oldfield worked out the developmental bugs and drove the car to an impressive string of victories. In duels with arch-rival Ralph DePalma's big 12-cylinder Packard, Oldfield won four races to DePalma's three. On August 9, 1917, at a one-mile oval in St. Louis, Missouri, the Golden Egg set new records for one mile at 80 mph; five miles at 77.2 mph; 25 miles at 75.4 mph; and 50 miles at 73.5 mph.

As Oldfield continued to set new records at nearly every board or dirt track on which he appeared, Harry Miller found himself suddenly and successfully in the race car business.

According to owner/restorer R. J. "Buck" Boudeman, at one point in the car's history

Miller and Oldfield had plans to put deflector wings on the car. Oldfield opined that if airplanes can be made to fly with wings, he ought to be able to use some sort of wing to hold the car on the track. As time would tell, Oldfield was about 50 years ahead of his time.

Clearly the most advanced race car of its day, the enclosed cockpit almost caused Oldfield's too-early demise. It caught fire in a bad crash at the Springfield, Illinois, Fairgrounds one-mile oval. When the car's single door jammed, Oldfield was trapped inside. With a mighty shove, the door finally opened and Oldfield dove for cover as the car's fuel tank exploded. When the car later reappeared, most of the "egg" had been cut away and Oldfield's now-famous and very radical machine looked more like the conventional race cars of the day.

On October 13, 1918, Barney Oldfield drove his last race, a sprint car event at Independence, Missouri. The "King of Speed" spent his remaining years as a spokesman for the automotive industry, promoting driving safety. Harry Miller went on to build a series of magnificent cars that dominated the American racing scene throughout the mid-1920s to the late 1930s. This Barney Oldfield 1917 Golden Sub is a re-creation.

1925 Duesenberg 122

Fred and August (Augie) Duesenberg were more than just brothers in business together; they were a designing and manufacturing team. Fred was the creator and innovator, the engineer who dreamed up new ideas. Augie was the machinist and builder, who turned Fred's sketches and drawings into working pieces of sheet metal and aluminum. It is difficult to imagine how successful one brother might have been without the other.

The 1925 Indianapolis 500 brought together two cars in this book: this 1925 Duesenberg and the 1925 Miller front-drive. Seventy-two years later they're going at it again at the Miller Club event on the Milwaukee Mile. *David Uihlein Collection*

In 1924 the Duesenberg brothers introduced the supercharger to American racing and won the Indy 500. But 1925 was the banner year for the brothers Duesenberg. In what may have been one of the greatest Indy races ever, the Duesenbergs entered the same car that had won in 1924. It was a 122-ci, supercharged straight-eight with Pete DePaolo at the wheel. Among the competitors was a shocking number of Millers, including the first Miller front-drive car.

In a report to the CompuServe On-Line Motorsports Forum, vintage race car historian Chris Etzel writes, "The pedigree of this car is amazing. It's the first car on a very short list of cars that have won the Indy 500 not once, but twice! Driving what was to prove the most famous of all Duesenberg racers, Peter DePaolo won the 1925 Indianapolis 500 and became the first driver to average over 100 mph for the race distance."

The car is also notable as the first car to use the new Firestone Balloon tires. These wider tires ran at much lower pressure than previous racing tires and offered better traction on the rough racing surfaces of the day. Firestone Tire & Rubber Co. made a major advance in racing tires by replacing the narrow-cord-carcass, high-pressure tires used since the early days. The Firestone Balloon tires were wider in cross section with more flexible sidewalls and ran at much lower pressure—30 psi rather than the 50 to 90 psi required by traditional tires.

It was DePaolo's year. He was also victorious on the board tracks at Fresno, California; Altoona, Pennsylvania; Laurel, Maryland; and Salem, New Hampshire. He earned the 1925 AAA National Championship.

At the end of the 1926 season the Duesenberg brothers sold the car to Bill White who put dirt track star George Souders behind the wheel. Souders proceeded to win the 1927 Indianapolis 500 in his rookie year at the Brickyard.

The car is restored to its 1925 specifications, wearing the bright yellow paint that record books of the day called "banana" and caused Peter DePaolo to call it "the Banana Wagon."

The supercharged Miller 122 had bodywork just slightly wider than the driver's shoulders and was so low-slung that even veteran racers gaped in amazement. Pit wall "experts" joked that the driver's elbows might scrape the pavement. *David Uihlein Collection*

Dashboard gauges from left to right: tachometer, oil pressure, water temperature. Simple and uncluttered. *David Uihlein Collection*

THE ELEGANT MILLERS

1925 SUPERCHARGED MILLER 122 FRONT-DRIVE RED #21

Somewhere in a weather-beaten barn or the back of an old shop is a complete, unrestored Miller race car. A pencil-thin and purposeful car just waiting for a dedicated owner to return it to full song—with gleaming paint and plating, growling engine, and whining gearbox. Is it possible? Maybe. To date not every vintage Miller has been located or documented. Is it probable? No, but among Miller enthusiasts the dream persists.

However, there's an old saying: "Great race cars never die."

Recreation Red #21 may be the perfect example of this.

This was probably the second front-drive car Harry Miller built for the 1925 season. Its outboard-mounted front brakes are the major point of historic contention. All other Miller front-drives had inboard brakes on either side of the transmission. The first front-drive, with inboard brakes, the "Junior Eight" was built for Jimmy Murphy, under General Motors heir Cliff Durant's sponsorship.

This outboard brake car was supposed to be a factory team car for Bennett (Benny) Hill. According to the story, Miller built this outboard-brake car for team-driver Hill. During testing or qualifying at Indianapolis that spring, Hill reported handling problems with the car and asked Harry to withdraw it. Hill then proceeded to qualify in 13th position with a Miller rear-drive car #3.

In the race #3 fell out on lap 69 with a broken rear spring. Hill watched the race from the pits. At the 400 mile mark Benny replaced exhausted driver Dave Lewis in the Junior 8 car, the only front-drive Miller to make the race. By this time race leader Pete DePaolo, driving a heroic race in the blown Duesenberg "Banana Wagon," had a full lap on the field. Though the Miller pulled quickly through the turns and Hill was steadily gaining on leader DePaolo, the race ended too quickly for the low-slung front-drive car. DePaolo took the checkered flag with a half-lap lead over Hill.

Harry Miller later sold the car to the Packard Motor Car Co. for its research into front-wheel drive. They, in turn, sold it to a privateer Stan Reed who raced it only three or four times. Reed sold it to owner-driver Frank Brisko who modified it extensively over the years.

This 1925 Miller chassis was re-bodied by Myron Stevens and re-powered by Frank Brisko, with a six-cylinder engine of his own design. Driver Louis Tomei raced it through the 1946 AAA Championship season as the Boxar Tool entry.

Front-wheel drive was an idea pioneered by Walter Christie with his 1912 race car. Christie was never successful with his ugly and ill-handling experiment and sold it to Barney Oldfield who added the beast to his stable of barnstorming race cars. Resurrected and perfected by Harry Miller and Leo Goossen , front-drive designs campaigned on American oval tracks for the next 40 years. The Miller-Fords of 1935, Lou Moore's post-war Blue Crown Specials, and the infamous Novi's all used front-drive with varying degrees of success.

In theory, a car being pulled through a turn by its front wheels would corner faster and truer than one being pushed by its rear wheels. Like many racing-inspired ideas, front-drive looked good on paper, but was difficult to engineer and even more difficult to drive.

Without a driveshaft to the rear axle, front-wheel-drive cars could be built lower to the ground and both engine and driver sat lower between the frame rails. The advantages of a lower center of gravity and wind-cheating frontal area were offset by the fact that the steering was heavy and front-tire wear was a problem.

The idea was finally put to rest by the rear-engined cars of the 1960s when better suspensions and wide, sticky tires erased the need for complicated and expensive front-drive setups.

1927 MILLER 91 REAR-DRIVE "BOYLE VALVE SPECIAL"

For the 1926 season the International Grand Prix Formula was reduced to 91 cubic inches. America's AAA Contest Board followed along and Harry Miller responded with a 91-ci, supercharged, straight-eight—essentially a downsized Miller 122 engine. It produced 136 horsepower at 6,500 rpm on low-octane racing fuel that limited compression ratios to 8:1. By 1929 Miller was able to boost power to about 200 horsepower at 8,000 rpm with more efficient blower design.

Millers dominated big-league oval-track racing. And the Miller-Duesenberg rivalry continued. For the 1927 Indianapolis 500, Millers filled all but five of the 33 starting positions. Those five were Duesenbergs. Rookie George Souders put a Duesey on the pole at 111.551 miles per hour. Souders went on to win the race. He was the first rookie in Indianapolis history to do so.

Cliff Woodbury drove this Miller 91 rear-drive in the 1927 Indianapolis 500. He started in sixth place then dropped out on lap 108 with supercharger troubles.

With limited success, Harry Miller would go on to design more advanced and exotic race cars and successful marine engines, but it was

Cliff Woodbury drove this Miller 91 rear-drive in the 1927 Indianapolis 500. He started in sixth place then dropped out on lap 108 with supercharger troubles.

these little 1.5-liter "Miller 91s" that escalated him to the pantheon of automotive history.

Still an award winner, this re-creation Miller 91 rear-drive car won *Automobile Quarterly* Magazine's Historic Award at Pebble Beach in 1995. It also won the Peter Helck Award for Best Open Wheel Car at the Meadowbrook Concours in 1996.

1927 MILLER REAR-DRIVE "PERFECT CIRCLE"

In the 1927 Indianapolis race Frank Lockhart put Miller on the pole at 120.100 miles per hour, but did not finish due to a broken connecting rod.

A brilliant self-taught engineer as well as heroic driver, Lockhart frequently quarreled with Miller over his improvements to Harry's masterful engineering. Lockhart is credited with the invention of the intercooler, which further boosted the horsepower of supercharged engines by cooling the superheated air before it entered the combustion chamber.

This example is a recreation of the one driven by Frank Lockhart. The current owner, Chuck Davis started with Lockhart's original intercooler for the supercharger and made a new body and frame for it. The engine is a Miller but isn't the original one used in this particular car. Most other parts are original Miller pieces from a variety of other cars.

In the 1927 Indianapolis race Frank Lockhart put the 1927 Miller on the pole at 120.100 mph, but did not finish due to a broken connecting rod. Lightweight aluminum discs were a trick used to eliminate the air turbulence created by wire wheels. *Chuck Davis Collection*

Firestone's Balloon tires were the first major breakthrough in racing tires. Their flexible sidewalls and low inflation pressure of 30 psi allowed better traction and handling on the rough racing surfaces of the day. *Mitchell Rasansky Collection*

By the late 1920s suspension basics were well established: four-wheel hydraulic brakes, leaf springs all around, and simple, friction-type shock absorbers. *Robert Sutherland Collection*

Along with engineering excellence, Harry Miller's cars were known—and owners paid handsomely—for their impeccable fit and finish. It was an obsession with Miller. *Robert Sutherland Collection*

1929 MILLER 91 REAR-DRIVE "MAJESTIC SPECIAL"

The beautiful "Majestic Special" Miller ran the 1929 season with the famous Lou Moore behind the wheel. It was sponsored by the Majestic Radio Company.

This re-creation car is an example of why Harry Miller's cars were admired not only for their performance but also for their impeccable fit and finish. Miller bought few components or sub-assemblies from outside suppliers. Almost

Even with wider two-man bodies to meet the 1930 AAA rules, Millers retained their distinctive lines.
Chuck Davis Collection

every piece of his racers were built in his own factory, by his own people, who understood and respected Miller's attention to detail. His employees, including Fred Offenhauser, Myron Stevens, and others, were as much artisans as machinists and fabricators.

This car has the engine and transmission from the original Majestic Radio car. Owner Bob Sutherland can attest to the thrill of getting behind the wheel of this car. There's plenty of power, he says. It has a three-speed transmission, but the final-drive ratio is pretty tall because Sutherland built it to possibly run at Indianapolis again someday. He runs it most of the time in second gear, peaking out at about 6,500 rpm.

1932 MILLER V-16 REAR DRIVE

Engine design changed after 1929, the final year of the demanding 91-ci rules. For the 1930 season engines could be as large as 366 cubic inches and superchargers were banned. The onset of the Great Depression saw a great deal of mechanical creativity substituting for dollars.

The Miller V-16 engine was the result of joining two Miller straight-eights on a common crankcase. Driver Shorty Cantlon threw a rod in this car during the 1931 Indy 500 race. In the 1932 Indianapolis 500, Bryan Saulpaugh finished 32nd in a field of 40 cars.

By the early 1930s, tires were growing wider in cross-section. These treadless Firestones were an early attempt to get more rubber to the pavement—"racing slicks." *Chuck Davis Collection*

Now owned by Chuck Davis, the re-created car had been re-bodied with bulbous Maserati-styled sheet metal. As late as 1948, the car had tried to run the AAA Championship series. The engine came from Bill Smith's collection in Lincoln, Nebraska. It had been cut in half by the late, great, Miller- and Offy-engine expert Joe Gemsa to use as a sprint car engine. When the original engine patterns were found, the necessary new pieces were cast to make a complete engine.

Gemsa restored the engine in 1988.

According to Davis, Harry Miller's cams had very little overlap, so it's a very smooth-running automobile. The car has an on-board starter as it did in 1932 and, with three speeds and reverse, it's a very driveable race car.

1932 MILLER "FWD" FOUR-WHEEL DRIVE

The products of Harry Miller's mystic creativity, Leo Goossen's brilliant design, and Fred Offenhauser's precision metal working were so fast, so good, so expensive, and so precious they were raced season after season, year after year, long past anyone's reasonable expectation of a useful racing career.

The fabulous Millers of the 1920s raced into the years of the Great Depression, when even the wealthiest teams narrowly escaped financial ruin. To keep racing, teams repaired, reused, and re-machined what they had. They begged, borrowed, and bartered for what they didn't have. These were the years of "patch and paint to match."

As with so many Millers, this car—a 308-ci V-8—campaigned many years and was driven by many drivers.

In the 1932 Memorial Day Classic, with its original Miller 308-ci V-8, this car was entered by the Four Wheel Drive Automobile Company. Driver Bob McDonough started 24th and finished 38th, with a broken oil line. Its best year at Indianapolis was 1936, with Mauri Rose driving. The car finished fourth.

This car shows an advancement in Miller's thinking about suspension: upper and lower quarter-elliptic springs front and rear. The innovation can also seen on the 1932 V-16 car. Adjustable friction shocks were more commonly used. *Dean Butler Collection*

This 255-ci Miller four-cylinder engine replaced the original, and more troublesome, 303-ci V-8. *Dean Butler Collection*

In the 1932 Memorial Day Classic, it was entered by the Four Wheel Drive Automobile Company. Driver Bob McDonough started 24th and finished 38th after suffering a broken oil line. Its best year at Indianapolis was 1936. With Mauri Rose driving, the car finished fourth.

The Miller V-8 never performed up to expectations. The lubrication system was troublesome. For the 1934 season new operator Frank Brisko switched to a Miller 255-ci four-cylinder engine. Brisko worked for the FWD, Company in Clintonville, Wisconsin, which owned the Miller FWD car. After Harry Miller's bankruptcy in 1934, Brisko was able to salvage the basic engine castings. These were combined with moving parts specially machined by Fred Offenhauser. From these humble beginnings, this car proceeded to make history.

A Leo Goossen-designed transfer case mated with the three-speed transmission fed power to both front and rear axles. It proved troublesome, but when it worked, the four-wheel-drive car demonstrated improved traction on Indy's rough brick surface.

In 1948, its oval-track career ended, and the Four Wheel Drive Motor Company loaned this car to Sports Car Club of America (SCCA) driver Bill Milliken for research and development on other projects. He competed in the 1948 Pikes Peak Hillclimb and at the 1949 Watkins Glen road races. In 1950 Milliken won the Mount Equinox Hill Climb in addition to other New England road races and hillclimbs. Not bad for an 18-year-old car!

Milliken remembers, "The car suffered from trailing-throttle oversteer. Easing off the throttle going into a corner made the back get loose. It wasn't too bad, but you really had to stay on top of it."

Millers, in all their variations, were the greatest race cars of their day. Dean Butler, owner of this authentic 1932 Miller "FWD" Four-Wheel Drive, says, "I believe collectors like myself are more like conservators of these cars and their history. I think it's important to get them into running condition and maintain them that way, so they can be seen and enjoyed as they actually were."

Cars like this Model T "Special" (a common term in those days for any home-built car) ran in the teens and 1920s on dirt tracks from Maine to Southern California. *Ken & Joan Gierach*

Model Ts were pivotal cars in American racing. They increased the size of the sport by making racing affordable and they increased gate receipts as spectators came out to see their local heros. *Ken & Joan Gierach*

SPRINT CARS

1920s MODEL T SPECIAL

When Henry Ford introduced the Model T in 1909, he not only put working-class America on the road, he put working-class America on the racetrack. Car owners with fat wallets could afford Duesenbergs, exotic foreign machinery, and Millers. Racers in the hinterlands relied on the ubiquitous Model T.

Using just the engine, driveline, frame, and suspension, the Model T was a lightweight, nimble, sturdy, simple, and relatively inexpensive racing machine. Front suspension used the Model T's solid I-beam axle, suspended from a leaf spring mounted across the front frame horns (cross-spring suspension), controlled by friction shock absorbers. The Ford solid rear axle also used the cross-spring arrangement and was located by a single torque tube drive located by rear radius rods and friction shock-absorber on each side.

It wasn't very sophisticated, but it was easily understood by the self-taught mechanics of that era. Equally important, this solid-axle suspension worked well on dirt tracks. With only slight refinement over the next decades, this suspension system would carry sprint cars for the next 70 years. With aftermarket heads by Frontenac, Rajo, or Gallivan, in single- or double-overhead-cam versions, these cars were surprisingly quick and exciting.

Cars like this Model T "Special" (a common term in those days for any home-built car) ran in the teens and 1920s on dirt tracks from Maine to Southern California.

Model Ts were pivotal cars in American racing. They increased the size of the sport by making racing affordable and they increased gate receipts as spectators came out to see their local heros.

The term "sprint car" didn't come into use until after World War II. Prior to that they were called "big cars" to separate them from the midgets of the 1930s and 1940s. They were sometimes called "three-quarter cars" to separate them from the larger and faster machines that campaigned the AAA Championship Trail of one-mile dirt tracks.

This "T" Special features a Waukesha high-compression head and Winfield racing carburetor.

With its dropped front axle, rounded radiator shell, and ~~boat-tail stern, this low-slung racer defies the~~ criticism that Frontys were boxy and homely *Robert McConnell Collection*

Owner of this re-created Model T Special, Ken Gierach claims a top speed of 60 miles per hour with the engine now producing 45 to 50 horsepower instead of its original 20 horsepower.

1923 FRONTY-FORD

While not as glamorous or expensive as the Duesenbergs or Millers of the day, Louis, Arthur, and Gaston Chevrolet's Fronty-Fords are some of the most important cars in racing history. In the 1916 Indianapolis 500, brothers Louis and Arthur drove four-cylinder Frontenacs to 12th and 18th places. Then in the 1930

Indy 500, Chet Miller wheeled a two-man, Model T-engined Fronty-Ford to a respectable 13th place finish.

Fronty-Fords compiled an incredible record in dirt-track racing around the country. And like the Model T Specials, they brought racing within the financial reach of grassroots competitors.

Many of these grassroots drivers would go on to fame at Indianapolis; Langhorne, Pennsylvania; DuQuoin, Illinois; and other "big tracks" of the AAA Championship circuit. They would move on to bigger, fancier, more expensive machinery and more prize money, but they learned their craft on the quarter- and half-mile dirt ovals, broad-sliding through turns behind the wheel of a "Fronty."

By the 1930s cars and tracks like these had established themselves as the training ground for big-league American racing.

The Chevrolet brothers, operating as the Frontenac Company were early pioneers in the aftermar-

The famous Frontenac SOHC head conversion on a Model T block with two Winfield racing carbs was a hot setup in its day. *Robert McConnell Collection*

Fronty-Fords compiled an incredible record in dirt-track racing around the country. And like the Model T Specials, they brought racing within the financial reach of grassroots competitors. *Robert McConnell Collection*

This sprinter was driven by dirt-track greats including: Troy Ruttman, Pat O'Conner, Tony Bettenhausen, Ed Elisian, Bob McCoy, Jerry Hoytand, Cal Nyday, and many others.

ket speed-equipment business. In addition to their famous Fronty-Ford cylinder head conversions, they sold entire engines and it was even possible to get the engine with a supercharger. Complete cars were also offered in their catalog. The name Frontenac was used because by 1914, Louis had signed away to General Motors rights to the use of the Chevrolet name.

Owner and veteran collector Bob McConnell explains, "These cars were put together out of various components. They'd start out with a Model T frame and a Model T engine. Then they'd install the Frontenac head and Winfield or Miller carburetors. The sheet metal came from Morton & Brett, body-builders in Indianapolis at the time." This Fronty-Ford is an authentic original.

This particular car has a Frontenac single-overhead-cam (SOHC) head on a Model T block, with two Winfield Model S carburetors. It also has Buffalo brand wire wheels, which hints that this car was raced on the West Coast.

1950 FAMIGHETTI-KUZMA SPRINT CAR

Sprint cars and sprint-car racing have never been subjected to the frequent rule changes that advanced technology at the highest level of racing, such as at Indianapolis and the other tracks comprising the Championship Trail. However, by the 1950s even the tradition-loving sprint cars had abandoned the twisty, two-rail frames for the stiffer tubular-frame chassis.

Representative of late-1940s and 1950s sprint/dirt track cars, this car has cross-spring suspension front and rear, wire wheels, friction shocks all around, and the traditional nose piece of the era with the small oval grille. Rear brakes only are hydraulic drum and shoe. *John Ryals Collection*

Retaining the curving lines and rounded bodywork of earlier generations, this mid-1960s-vintage sprinter also displays the integral roll cage, which wasn't widely accepted in dirt-track racing until the early 1970s. It also wears the wider rear tires of later years. *Bob Moore Collection*

By the early 1950s, rear-only brakes were now hydraulic as were the shock absorbers, but the cars retained the solid front- and rear-axle, dirt-track suspension and the upright seating position mandated by the exposed driveshaft running under the driver's seat.

Black #88 is a West Coast car that competed for more than 20 years in sprint competition with the San Diego Racing Association. It may be one of the last rail-frame cars to be built after World War II.

This authentic sprinter was driven by many dirt track greats including: Troy Ruttman, Pat O'Conner, Tony Bettenhausen, Ed Elisian, Bob McCoy, Jerry Hoytand, and Cal Niday. This is the only race car that driver Troy Ruttman ever owned. For the rest of his career he drove cars owned by others.

Legendary Southern California car-builder Eddie Kuzma built the body panels, but Charlie, Jim, and Ted Famighetti built the chassis and the original six-cylinder Chrysler powerplant. For the 1952 season they replaced the Chrysler with a 270 Offenhauser, the mainstay engine of post-war racing.

1965 MESKOWSKI-CHEVY

Abrasive, relentlessly competitive, and brutally critical of his own drivers, Wally Meskowski, nevertheless, built great sprint cars. At one time or another, most of the great oval-track stars of this era spent time at the cockpit of one of his sprint cars—Mario Andretti, Johnny Rutherford, and Bud Tinglestad are among them.

The first small-block V-8 rolled off Chevrolet's Detroit assembly line in the 1955 models, and by 1958 clever racing-engine builders recognized the horsepower potential of this inexpensive, readily available, stock-block motor. By the 1960s aftermarket machine shops offered an amazing variety of hop-up equipment that turned the Chevy into a powerful, dependable racing engine. By 1965 the larger Chevy V-8 had replaced the venerable, but expensive, Offenhauser four-bangers. Meskowski quickly incorporated this new powerplant into his cars.

Sprint car specifications were well established. They had a wheelbase of 84 inches, a minimum tread width of 47 inches and a minimum weight of 1,400 pounds. The machines that evolved around those measurements were considered to be the meanest, most difficult to drive, most overpowered and exciting cars in oval-track history. Many feel that's still true today.

These cars were built around two principles: they had to be simple and they had to be tough. The weekly pounding these cars endured on the rutted bull rings of sprint-car racing would have destroyed lesser machinery.

By 1965 sprint cars and midgets had evolved into an unparalleled form of racing. In big-league racing—then called the United States Auto Club (USAC) Championship racing—the roadster revo-

Sprint cars were considered to be the meanest, trickiest handling, most overpowered and exciting cars in oval track history. Many feel that's still true today.

lution of the 1950s was followed by the rear-engine funny car revolution of the 1960s. That evolution brought an end to the traditional dual-purpose, dirt-and-pavement, upright race cars that ran so successfully during the early post-war years.

Few drivers with broad-sliding, mud-slinging, dirt-track experience were considered able to handle the twitchy, oh-so-delicate, rear-engined cars.

Most of the big one-mile ovals had been paved, and in 1970 USAC sealed the fate of dirt-track racing with its decision to no longer recognize points earned on dirt tracks.

Racing under both United States Auto Club (USAC) and International Motor Contest Association (IMCA) sanctions, this authentic and original red and yellow #56 saw action on tracks throughout the Midwest before retiring in the early 1970s.

The ELTO 460 Midget had a 460-ci flat four-cylinder engine mounted vertically in the engine compartment. It drives the rear wheels with a right-angle gear drive through an in-out box to the rear end. This particular car was never raced. *Tom Sturm Collection*

In the midst of the Great Depression a new kind of car and a new kind of racing emerged. Midgets were scaled-down versions of dirt-track cars. The sport grew from home-built hobby cars for kids that were raced in local club events. *Tom Sturm Collection*

THE MIDGETS ARRIVE

1930s ELTO 460 MIDGET

In the midst of the Great Depression a new kind of car and a new kind of racing emerged. The cars were scaled-down versions of dirt-track cars. They were called "midgets." The sport grew from home-built hobby cars for kids that were raced in local club events. Apparently a few adults thought the kids were having entirely too much fun.

Beginning in 1933 there were loosely organized races in Southern California and on the East Coast. Then in 1934, Earl Gilmore, of Gilmore Oil Co. fame, built his 18,500-seat Los Angeles quarter-mile dirt oval specifically for midgets. Driven by professional drivers from the big-car ranks, the tiny cars were officially recognized. The racing was wheel-to-wheel. Flips, spins, and crashes punctuated every race and the fans loved it. Midget racing went from locally popular to become a national craze.

By 1935 midgets were racing coast-to-coast on existing half-mile dirt tracks, hastily bulldozed quarter-mile tracks, 1/5-mile board ovals bolted together inside auditoriums, and on high school running tracks circling the football fields.

During their heyday the tiny cars added another aspect to the world of motor racing—a third, bottom-most rung to the "career ladder" leading to a chance at an Indy ride. Duke Nalon, Tony Bettenhausen, Bill Vukovich, and A.J. Foyt are just a few of the famous names who worked their way up this ladder.

Early midgets used a variety of small engines that were cheap and readily available. One of the most popular was a two-cycle motor adapted from the small-boat industry.

The two-cycle ELTO 460 was the abbreviated terminology for the Evinrude Light Twin Outboard motor, an air-cooled, horizontally opposed four-cylinder engine rated at 60 horsepower. That's not much horsepower, but then a lot of these cars only weighed 500 pounds. This 1930s ELTO 460 Midget is an authentic original.

Midget car racing was wheel-to-wheel. Flips, spins, and crashes punctuated every race and the fans loved it. This beautifully restored ELTO 460 was photographed at the Del Mar, California, vintage race car show.

Early midgets used a variety of small engines that were cheap and readily available. One of the most popular was a two-cycle motor adapted from the small-boat industry. ELTO 460 was the common term for an Evinrude Light Twin Outboard, an air-cooled, horizontally opposed, four-cylinder engine rated at 60 horsepower.

1930s HARLEY-DAVIDSON SPECIAL

The Harley-Davidson motorcycle V-twin was another favorite engine for early midgets. They were lightweight and powerful for their size. Dale Drake, later of Meyer-Drake-Offenhauser fame, had some success with water-cooled conversions of these engines. Leo Goossen redesigned the Harley for Drake with a beefed-up crankshaft and new water-cooled cylinders.

The problem with both these and the ELTOs was unreliability. They were finicky about fuel/air mixtures, hard to start, and smoked profusely—not a good combination for indoor racing. The 2-cycle ELTOs (generally known only as outboards), in addition to being hard to start, tended to foul spark plugs readily. Race promoters, car owners, and mechanics went looking for a better answer.

Within a few years powerplants evolved through the Ford flathead V-8 and the Offenhauser "Mighty

This car varies from "authenticity" in that it has the cross-spring front suspension typical for cars of the period, but also has tubular hydraulic shock absorbers, which weren't invented until the early 1950s.

Midget." The post-war years brought a variety of souped-up Detroit in-line fours and, for a while during the 1970s, the Volkswagen flat four was a cheap and fast alternative to the expensive Offys. This 1930s Harley-Davidson Special is an authentic original.

1946 KURTIS-KRAFT FORD V-8 MIDGET

At the close of World War II, Frank Kurtis revolutionized American race cars with his famous tube-frame construction and torsion-bar suspension. For the first time, race car chassis were so torsionally rigid that the art of suspension tuning became important. His original experiments led to building midgets practically on a production-line basis.

Over the years other builders such as Gertler, Trevis, Dreyer, and Edmunds competed with Kurtis for a piece of the midget business and some of the fame. Kurtis enjoyed success with bigger cars, on bigger tracks, but he is remembered as the godfather of midget race cars.

What the OHV Chevy V-8 was to sprint cars, the Ford flathead V8-60 was to midgets—a less pricey alternative to the established Offenhausers. This stock-block engine became a racing favorite because of the ready supply of relatively inexpensive bolt-on speed equipment. This equipment could double and triple the engine's original horsepower. There were no speed secrets to the Ford flathead, everybody knew the tricks.

Though rarely as fast as Offy-powered cars, the cheaper V8-60s paved the way for many drivers to move up to classic machinery.

Eric Leider's neo-vintage midget is a 1946–47-style Kurtis midget powered by a Ford flathead V8-60 engine. This is a 1940s-style racer built in the 1990s by Arlen Kurtis, heir to his father's legend and a fine car builder in his own right.

Frank Kurtis revolutionized American race cars with his famous tube-frame construction and torsion-bar suspension. This is a 1940s-style racer built in the 1990s by Arlen Kurtis, heir to his father's legend and a fine car builder in his own right.

Properly tweaked and in a competitive chassis the flathead Ford V-8 could run pretty well against the all-conquering Offys. *Eric Leider Collection*

1948 KURTIS-OFFY

Midget racing peaked in 1948 with roughly two million tickets sold. The quintessential midget was the Kurtis-Kraft Offenhauser. From the earliest acceptance of midgets as real racing cars, those using Offenhauser engines won the majority of events where they were allowed to compete. So clearly out-running the rest of the field, Offys usually were run in their own class.

In 1935 ex-Harry Miller wizard Fred Offenhauser (who took over Miller's failed business) and Leo Goossen hit on the idea of powering midgets with the front half of a Miller 183-ci straight-eight engine. The

The quintessential midget was the Kurtis-Kraft Offenhauser. Today, when people talk of the great midgets of yesteryear, this is the image that comes to mind. *Junior Dreyer Collection*

Fred Offenhauser and Leo Goossen hit on the idea of powering midgets with the front half of a Miller straight-eight. The four-cylinder engines could be made cheaply, using existing patterns, and the basic engineering was sound. The small Offy-powered cars were dubbed "Mighty Midgets." *Junior Dreyer Collection*

Floyd Trevis built this roadster-style midget. Trevis down-sized the popular Indy roadsters of the day. *Jim and Dolores Hoersting Collection*

97-ci four-cylinder engines could be made cheaply using existing patterns. The basic engineering was sound.

The small four-cylinder Offy—dubbed the "Mighty Midget"—became famous in its own right, and helped put Offenhauser Engineering in the black as Fred Offenhauser rescued what was left of Harry Miller's bankrupt shop. This is an authentic original which was restored by the infamous Junior Dreyer. Junior learned the restoration trade from his father, Pop Dreyer, who built his own race cars.

1956 TREVIS MIDGET ROADSTER

This roadster-style midget is from car builder Floyd Trevis. His cars were essentially down-sized versions of the popular Indy roadsters. This particular car was raced unsuccessfully and finally parked. Roadsters never worked well as midgets on dirt tracks. However, they are significant in the fact that they were magnificent failures.

Roadster midgets were an attempt to gain the same advantages of their big brothers: low center of gravity and offset driveline weight. It worked on pavement, but not on dirt. *Jim and Dolores Hoersting Collection*

Many racing enthusiasts think the roadster midgets were ruled out of existence—not true! Their demise could be attributed to a high percentage of dirt tracks that remained on each racing circuit. Midget roadsters were built for paved tracks and did not run well on dirt. The roadster midgets didn't have the dual-purpose, asphalt or clay, flexibility of traditional upright midgets. This 1956 Trevis Midget Roadster is an authentic original.

NEXT
Set up for actual vintage racing, this midget wears treadless pavement tires, except for the front left which spends most of its time freewheeling in the air.

Midgets like this Kurtis-Offy served as stepping stones for grassroots racers. Some drivers who took this route included Tony Bettenhausen, Lloyd Ruby, Parnelli Jones, A.J. Foyt, Johnny Rutherford, and Mario Andretti.

1960s KURTIS-OFFY

By 1960 USAC had well-established specifications for the Kurtis-Kraft and all other midgets: wheelbase, 76 inches; tread, 50 inches; wheels, 13 inches in diameter and eight inches wide; roll bars or roll cages were mandatory. On pavement midgets used racing slicks. On dirt they used wide-treaded tires on the rear and front right, and a narrow tire on the left, front wheel. Because of chassis flex in the turns, this tire spent most of its time off the ground.

Throughout their history, midgets utilized the current sprint-car technology, simply scaled down to a 76-inch wheelbase. In the 1930s when sprint cars used rail frame chassis and friction shock absorbers, so did the midgets of the day. In the post-war period when sprint cars moved to tube frame chassis, Offenhauser engines, and torsion bars, so did the midgets. As sprint cars moved into the decade of the 1970s and the Offenhauser engine had raced its last race, midgets as well as sprint cars sought other power sources. And, while there has been many different powerplants used over the years besides the Offy, midgets, like sprint cars, were insulated from the expensive, high-tech innovation of their bigger brothers on the Indy car championship circuit. This is an authentic, original car.

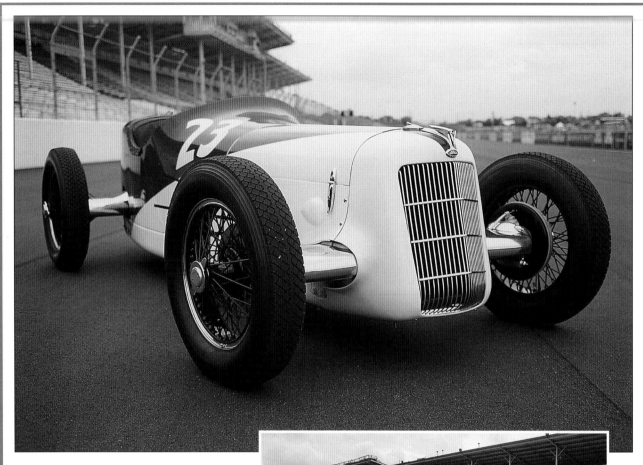

Though hurriedly designed and assembled under a short deadline, the Miller-Fords were some of the most beautiful cars to compete during the "Junk Formula" years. Note the streamlining panels over the front and rear axles. *Chuck Davis Collection*

Henry Ford insisted that Harry Miller incorporate a Ford passenger car grille in the design for product identification. *Chuck Davis Collection*

From Junk Formula to World War II

1935 MILLER-FORD

Even during the high-flying, easy-money days of the Roaring '20s, big-time championship racing was expensive. A Miller 91 rear-drive car cost $10,000 and a front-drive car cost $15,000. One of Miller's sophisticated engines alone cost $5,000.

Many people, including Eddie Rickenbacker who bought the Indianapolis Motor Speedway in 1927, were convinced that racing was too expensive. In their opinion, the rise of exotic, specialized race cars had taken American racing too far from one of its original purposes: a testing and proving ground for automobile manufacturers.

After two years of deliberation, the AAA Contest Board announced new rules for the 1930 season: superchargers were disallowed, the maximum engine displacement was increased to 366 cubic

Flathead Ford V-8 engines were mounted backwards in the chassis to drive the front wheels of the Miller-Fords. *Chuck Davis Collection*

inches, only two valves per cylinder were allowed, car weight was increased from 1,400 pounds to 1,750 pounds (minimum) with two-seat bodies, and riding mechanics were mandatory.

The rule change was partially successful. It encouraged participation, directly or indirectly, from American passenger car manufacturers: Studebaker, Buick, Stutz, Chrysler, and Ford. Preston Tucker encouraged Henry Ford to hire Harry Miller to design and build an all-new race car powered with a flathead Ford V-8. It was Tucker's stunt to advertise Ford's new passenger car engine.

In 1935 the Harry Miller/Ford team arrived in Indianapolis with ten hastily prepared cars, five primary cars, and five backups. This car driven by George Barringer didn't qualify for the 1935 race. Only four of the 10 Miller-Fords actually qualified and those four failed to finish because of the same steering-gearbox problem, proving that even the genius of a Harry Miller is sometimes flawed.

A few of these Miller-Fords would reappear in later years in various reincarnations. The engines and some parts of the bodywork were changed. The cars were repainted, given different numbers, and were put back on the track again. The 1941 Novi/Winfield and Andy Granatelli 1947 Grancor Special are two such examples. This 1935 Miller-Ford is an authentic original.

It would be 28 years before Ford Motor Co. officially returned to Indy in 1963 with their factory-backed Lotus-Fords.

1938 MASERATI 8CTF

During the years from 1930 to 1941 in American racing, significant technological change came slowly. The country was still struggling out of the Great Depression. As a result, most cars enjoyed uncommonly long careers, returning season after season with different teams, different drivers, different paint schemes, even different engines.

In 1938 the AAA Contest Board once again adopted International Grand Prix rules to lure well-

Clearly an engineering generation ahead of American competition when it arrived in this country, Automobili Maserati chassis #3030 first appeared at Indianapolis in 1940. *Dean Butler Collection*

The low-slung, single-seaters were powered by a 3.0-liter, 183-ci straight-eight with double-overhead cams and a two-stage, gear-driven, Roots supercharger producing 15-psi boost. Maserati claimed 350 horsepower at 6,500 rpm on 80 percent methanol. *Dean Butler Collection*

tracks. A few Alfa-Romeos joined the Maseratis, all under American ownership. No European factory teams made the trip across the Atlantic.

Wilbur Shaw's 1939 Indy win in a Maserati 8CTF, chassis number 3032, encouraged Lucy O'Reilly Schell to bring her two Maseratis, chassis numbers 3030 and 3031, to America for the 1940 season. Blue #49 is chassis #3030.

Clearly an engineering generation ahead of American competition when it arrived in this country, Automobili Maserati chassis #3030 first appeared at Indianapolis in 1940 and campaigned for 11 years, until it was wrecked during a qualifying run. Stunningly beautiful and sophisticated, the Maseratis introduced independent suspension and torsion bars to the oval-track crowd.

The low-slung, single-seaters were powered by a 3.0-liter, 183-ci straight-eight, with double-overhead cams and a two-stage, gear-driven, Roots supercharger, producing 15-psi boost. Maserati claimed 350 horsepower at 6,500 rpm on 80 percent methanol. This was about 100 horsepower more than the non-supercharged Offys. More importantly, the Roots-type superchargers didn't lose as much boost pressure in the turns as the American centrifugal blowers did. This gave them a better jump accelerating out of the corners.

In the 1940 Indy 500, chassis #3030 finished 10th, co-driven by Rene LeBegue and Rene Dreyfus. In 1941 both ex-Schell Maseratis raced as Elgin Piston Pin Specials driven by Duke Nalon and Mauri Rose. In 1946, the #3030 chassis (car #25) driven by Russ Snowberger did not finish. In the 1947 Indy 500 running as the Federal Engineering Special, with Snowberger again at the wheel, the car started 6th and finished 19th, going out on lap 74 with oil-pump problems. In the 1948 Indianapolis 500, still as the Federal Engineering Special, Paul Russo started in 25th position and finished 32nd with an oil leak. In 1949 Sam Hanks failed to qualify the car. In 1950, as the Fadely-Andersen Special, chassis #3030 was re-

powered with a 270 Offy. Driven by Spider Webb, it finished 20th.

In 1951 Bud Sennett, trying to qualify the car for the Auto Accessories Company, spun off Indy's southwest turn. The car rolled and hit a tree. Sennett walked away, but the Maserati was finished.

One of the Maseratis' strong points was their huge, hydraulic, four-wheel vented drum brakes designed for European road courses. The Maseratis weren't much faster down the straights, but relying on their brakes they could drive deeper into the corners.

The cars' weak point was the long 5-inch stroke of the engine. With Indianapolis' sustained high-rpm laps, the engines were hard on connecting rods and main bearings, particularly at the factory-specified red line of 6,500 rpm. Maserati blew engines with alarming frequency, but Wilbur Shaw's brilliant mechanic, Cotton Henning, geared Shaw's car to top out at 6,000 rpm. At 500 rpm below redline, Shaw's engine could run all day—and it did. This car is an authentic original.

1941 NOVI/WINFIELD

Immediately following their humiliating performance in the 1935 Indianapolis 500, Henry Ford padlocked all of his ill-fated Miller-Fords behind closed doors. However, over the next several years a few of the original 10 were quietly released to other owners. Veteran campaigner Lew Welch, from the Detroit suburb of Novi, Michigan, whose business was selling re-manufactured Ford engines, was a personal friend of Henry Ford and was apparently granted a special favor. In 1939 Cliff Bergere drove a re-bodied, Offy 270-powered Miller-Ford to 3rd place at Indianapolis for Welch.

In the 1947 Memorial Day 500, a young Andy Granatelli fielded a Miller-Ford with a slightly modified driver-only cockpit for Pete Romcevich. It raced as the "Camco Motors Ford." Pete qualified in 17th position and finished 12th. Not bad for a 12-year-old car.

One of the ill-fated 1935 Miller-Fords made a second appearance in the 1941 Indy carrying the Winfield brothers powerful supercharged V-8, the first in a long line of cars that carried the Novi name. *Bob Sutherland Collection*

Welch's authentic, second Miller-Ford chassis appears here, carrying the first of the renowned Winfield/Novi supercharged V-8s. In one of the better finishes of this engine's dramatic career, Rex Mays started and finished the 1941 Indianapolis 500 in second-place.

Futility is a word that best describes the history of the Novi engine. Ex-Miller designer Leo Goossen brought all his talent and experience to bear on this new engine. And while it always had great promise, the engine—in a variety of front-drive chassis by Frank Kurtis—was disappointing and deadly. Front-wheel-drive Novis and their weird handling characteristics took the lives of

Ralph Hepburn in 1948 and Chet Miller in 1953. Even the great Duke Nalon could never quite drive a Novi into the winner's circle.

For the next 20 years Lew Welch kept the Novi faith. It was never realized. Always the center of attention and controversy, the Novi broke the hearts of loyal fans. Year after year they cheered the sound of the screaming supercharged V-8 and rooted for this underdog engine to conquer the all-powerful Offenhausers, but it never happened.

All that would have to wait, however. Germany declared war on Europe, Japan declared war on the United States, and for the next three years all motor racing was suspended.

This car appears as it would have in 1946 livery when Mauri Rose drove it. The aluminum body was built by Ringling Bros. in Seattle, Washington. Bodywork stretched to enclose the front suspension is an early, simple attempt at smoothing the air flow around the car. *Don McReynolds Collection*

Joe Lencki built only three cars and he owned all three when he died, in 1994, at the age of 92. The engine from this car was in pieces on Lencki's workbench when he died, but the car was sitting on its original Firestone Deluxe Champion tires. *Don McReynolds Collection*

THE POST WAR YEARS

1946 "BLUE CROWN SPARK PLUG SPECIAL"

When American racing resumed in 1946 it used leftover pre-war machinery—much of it so old as to be laughable. This is one of many different cars campaigned under the sponsorship of the Blue Crown Spark Plug Co.

It was originally commissioned by Joe Lencki in 1937. The car was designed by Leo Goossen and built in 1938 by Fred Offenhauser. Six cylinders weren't the answer. It was a smooth-running engine, but plagued with minor problems. The four-cylinder Offys ran away from it. The horsepower increase resulting from two additional cylinders never made up for the increased weight of the six.

This car has both six-cylinder and four-cylinder engine mounts and ran the full AAA Championship circuit, possibly alternating between four- and six-cylinder engines as the car moved from track to track.

During the post-war years, as was true during and after the Depression, cars were built to compete year after year, not only at Indianapolis, but through a season of rough dirt ovals. This car is built tough and heavy, even by today's standards. There are no welds on the chassis; it is bolted together and the body is all riveted.

The car utilizes a traditional rail-frame chassis with cross-spring front and rear suspension controlled by lever-arm hydraulic shocks tucked inside the bodywork—an inboard mounting that was advanced for its day.

Blue Crown #8 carried another feature—four-wheel disc brakes. These worked more like a clutch system, with the two facing "clutch discs" pressed together by a single hydraulic cylinder. Harry Miller used this same, or similar, system on his ill-fated, but revolutionary, 1939 Gulf-Miller rear-engined cars.

This car ran the 1939 season with Tony Willman driving, in 1940 with George Conner at the wheel, and in 1941 with driver Emil Andres. Driven and wrecked by Mauri Rose in the 1946 Indy 500, the car came back in 1947 with Emil Andres driving. In 1948 and 1949 the car didn't make the field; it was taken back to Chicago and parked in Lencki's shop.

Joe Lencki built only three cars and he owned all three when he died in 1994 at the age of 92. When he died, the engine from this car was in pieces on Lencki's workbench, but the car was sitting on its original Firestone Deluxe Champion tires.

1949 LOU MOORE "BLUE CROWN SPARK PLUG SPECIAL"

There are two cars in this book that are in original, as-raced, unrestored condition. This car #7 is one of them. The chassis was built by Emil Deidt, the engine by Offenhauser, and the front-drive by Leo Goossen. This is one of two cars that team owner Lou Moore had specifically designed and built to run at Indy. He used conventional rear-drive cars to run the one-mile dirt ovals that comprised the rest of the AAA Championship Trail.

This #7 is an original, unrestored car. The chassis was built by Emil Deidt, the engine by Offenhauser, and the front-drive by Leo Goossen. *R. J. Buck Boudeman Collection*

Prior to the introduction of the roadster chassis, Lou Moore's Blue Crown Specials were some of the most beautiful and low-slung cars ever seen in racing. *R. J. Buck Boudeman Collection*

For driver Lou Moore was a meticulous planner. He brought all his knowledge to bear on a problem, made his plans, and stuck to them. Everyone knew the car making the fewest pit stops had the best chance of winning the race. Moore built on this idea.

The 270-ci, non-supercharged Offenhauser was the dominant engine of these years. Running on aviation gas it provided excellent fuel mileage. Moore believed front-drive was superior for Indy's pavement. He commissioned Leo Goossen to design a front-drive setup for the Offy and had Emil Deidt wrap a lightweight, low-slung, wind-cheating chassis and body around the whole works. The engine was modified for a very high compression ratio of 13:1, which at racing speeds delivered 12 miles to the gallon. It worked.

This car, making only one pit stop for fuel and tires, won Indy in 1949. It was driven by Bill Holland.

In the immediate post-war years, there was no one as successful, as dominant at Indy as team owner Lou Moore. His achievements included three championships in three years: 1947, 1948, and 1949.

Current owner, Buck Boudeman, discovered this car was at the company headquarters of the old Blue Crown Spark Plug Company and added #7 to his impressive collection.

1951 LUJIE LESOVSKY "BLUE CROWN SPECIAL"

Through the decades of the 1930s and 1940s, with the exception of Indianapolis Motor Speedway, all tracks on the Championship Trail

Car-builder Lujie Lesovsky built this car in 1951 for its original owner, Lindsey Hopkins. Typical of the Offy-powered, dual-purpose Championship Trail cars of the day, this car adopted Ted Halibrand's new magnesium wheels. *Don Lyons Collection*

were one-mile dirt ovals. Few owners could, or would, spend the money to have special cars built for Indy. Lou Moore and a few others were rare examples. The dual-purpose car was considered the cost-effective way to run the Trail.

Car-builder Lujie Lesovsky created this car in 1951 for its original owner Lindsey Hopkins—one of the great sportsman car owners of championship car racing for several decades. Lesovsky, along with Myron Stevens and Fred Offenhauser, were three race car builders who elevated automotive metal-working to an art form.

In this car, sitting behind one of the venerable 270-ci Offys, Henry Banks won the 1950 AAA Championship. Typical of many of the upright, dual-purpose cars of this era, this car spent most of its time on dirt tracks. When no longer competitive at Indy, it moved on to a long career in local and regional series.

Thirty-five years later, Lesovsky restored this original car for current owner Don Lyons of Dowagiac, Michigan. It was one of Lesovsky's last projects; he died in 1995.

1954 MYRON STEVENS CHASSIS "CHAPMAN SPECIAL"

A veteran of Harry Miller's racing shop during its heyday, Myron Stevens went on to build some of the most beautiful and successful American race cars of the 1940s and early 1950s. Stevens was in charge of Miller's sheet metal department. He was an artist with a welding torch. His cars were stiff and strong; his bodywork slick and sweeping.

Campaigned for a number of years with different drivers and paint schemes, the car is shown as it ran the 1954 season with Ed Elisian at the wheel.

Stevens started building this car in 1951 at his shop in Arizona. An argument between Stevens and Allan Chapman, the owner, resulted in the car being finished in 1952 in Frank Kurtis' California shop. Kurtis and race driver Bill Schindler did most of the final mechanical work.

Myron Stevens was a veteran of Harry Miller's racing shop during its heyday in the 1920s and 1930s. He went on to build some of the most beautiful and successful American race cars of the 1940s and early 1950s. *Joe Baird and Thomas E. Malloy collections*

Myron Stevens was in charge of Harry Miller's sheet metal department. He was an artist with a welding torch. His cars were stiff and strong, his bodywork slick and sweeping. Note the fairings and carefully machined details on the bodywork of this car. *Joe Baird and Thomas E. Malloy collections*

Race car technology at this time featured the unblown 270-ci Offy engine, solid axles front and rear, and leaf-spring suspension. This car also incorporated four-wheel, hydraulic disc brakes and the new magnesium wheels.

This is one of the nicest, and one of the last, examples of the upright Offy dual-purpose Indy/dirt track cars. This authentic, original car continued to race through the 1955, 1956, and 1957 seasons—well into the roadster era.

1957 KURTIS-KRAFT OFFY ROADSTER

Change occurs slowly in automobile racing; technological development occurs in small increments. Each new development builds upon lessons learned from the past. It is a process of evolution rather than revolution. But there are exceptions.

The Kurtis-Kraft roadsters of the 1950s were certainly the most revolutionary cars seen in 20 years and they would come to dominate paved ovals for the next ten years. They were never intended to run on dirt tracks.

Kurtis developed his first 500A roadster with input from mechanics Jim Travers and Frank Coons, later of Traco engine fame.

The high-riding, dual-purpose dirt/Indy cars were replaced by the Kurtis roadsters and later variations on the Frank Kurtis theme by A.J. Watson, Quinn Epperly, and Eddie Kuzma.

Originally built in 1953 for driver Jim Rathman, the car appears here in its 1957 livery, as owned by Ernest Ruiz and with rookie Elmer George as the driver. George would later wed Mary Hulman whose father, Tony, owned the Speedway. Elmer and Mary's son, Tony George, is now president of both the Speedway and the new Indianapolis Racing League.

With Ernest Ruiz as owner, this car first raced at Indy in 1953 with Jim Rathman driving. Rathman started 25th and finished seventh. The chassis is a Kurtis-Kraft 500B. This was the eighth roadster built by Frank Kurtis and the third 500B chassis.

In 1954 with Bob Scott driving, it was too slow to qualify. In 1955 with Bill Homeier driving, once again it was not fast enough to qualify. In 1956 with Jack Turner driving, the car qualified but developed engine trouble on lap 131 and finished 25th.

A new, single-file pace lap procedure was tried at Indy in 1957 and this car crossed wheels with Eddie Russo's #55 roadster on the parade lap.

Retired after the 1957 race, the car stayed with Ernest Ruiz until 1970 when it was sold to Tom Hillier. Terms of the sale included an agreement that it not be chopped up to make a super-modified chassis. This was the fate of most Kurtis-Kraft roadsters and helps explain why there are so few around today.

This 500B is a four-torsion-bar car with the front bars criss-crossed at an angle. It also has a solid-beam front axle, disc brakes on all four wheels, and the new upright Monroe tubular hydraulic shocks.

Current owner Philip Parnegian installed a 270 Offy with Hilborn fuel injection. The engine was rebuilt by the late, great, Offenhauser engine specialist Joe Gemsa. Gemsa set this engine up to run on ordinary pump gasoline, because alcohol requires daily maintenance and hastens the deterioration of rubber parts. The engine is laid over at 45 degrees. Although the driveline is offset 8 inches to the left, the car is not offset on the suspension. The offset-suspension concept would come with later variations on the roadster theme by A.J. Watson and other builders. The full belly-pan from front to rear, 75-gallon fuel tank, Hali-

With Ernest Ruiz as owner, this car first raced at Indy in 1953 with Jim Rathman driving. It started 25th and finished seventh. The chassis is a Kurtis-Kraft 500B. This was the eighth roadster built by Frank Kurtis and the third 500B chassis.

brand quick-change differential, and Scintilla-Vertex magneto were standard-issue racing items of the roadster era. The car sits on original 1950s-vintage tires, which don't encourage driving the car at high speeds.

This is the second of two unrestored "as raced" cars in this book. It's an extremely rare find in the world of vintage race cars that serves to fuel the ongoing collector's dream of finding perfectly complete automobiles sitting in someone's barn or garage.

1959 LEADER CARD WATSON/OFFY ROADSTER

When he burst onto the scene, Frank Kurtis' ideas were considered revolutionary, yet Kurtis was remarkably stubborn about changing what he believed to be the best way to build a pavement roadster. Meanwhile, master mechanic and crew chief A.J. Watson took the Kurtis roadsters one step further. He was the first to use the new coil-over shock absorber/spring combination. He kept the Offy engine upright, but further offset it 12 inches to the left, which was 3 inches more than the Kurtis design. Then he offset the entire frame and body 1 1/2 inches to the left.

By 1959 Watson's cars completely eclipsed the now-obsolete Kurtis-Kraft chassis.

This car is a re-creation of the Indy-winning #5 as driven by Roger Ward in 1959. It was assembled in 1991 by Roger Ward and his brother, with the help of A.J. Watsons.

The engine is laid over 45 degrees and offset eight inches to the left, but the car is not offset on the suspension—this would come with later variations on the roadster theme by A.J. Watson and other builders. *Phil Parnegian Collection*

This #5 car is a re-creation of the 1959 Indy-winner driven by Roger Ward. It was assembled in 1991 by Roger Ward and his brother, with the help of A.J. Watson. *Tom Malloy Collection*

In addition to chassis improvements A.J. Watson also refined the lines of the traditional roadster. Note the trademark Watson shark nose. *Tom Malloy Collection*

1962 A.J. WATSON LEADER CARD OFFY ROADSTER

This authentic car finished 2nd in the 1962 Indy 500 driven by veteran Len Sutton. It also raced at Indy in 1961 as a Leader Card #41, with Johnny Boyd as driver. In 1963 it was the Demler Special #99, with Paul Goldsmith driving. Then in 1964 it was the Demler Special, with Johnny White as driver. In 1965 Ralph Liguori drove it as the #99 Demler Special, but wrecked it in practice.

From there it went on (as did so many of the roadsters of this era) to race as a supermodified at Oswego, New York.

The Watson roadsters gained precedence over the Kurtis-Kraft roadsters as car owners saw the refinement that Watson brought to the basic roadster concept.

This roadster saw many different drivers and entry configurations. It raced at Indy in 1961 as a Leader Card #41, with Johnny Boyd as driver. In 1963 it was the Demler Spl. #99, with Paul Goldsmith driving. Then in 1964 it was the Demler Spl. with Johnny White as driver. *Robert McConnell Collection*

A.J. Watson's roadsters were longer, lighter and more aerodynamic than the original Kurtis-Krafts that established the roadster style. *Robert McConnell Collection*

1964 KUZMA-OFFY CHAMP CAR

Once driven by Mario Andretti, this authentic, original Eddie Kuzma version of the roadster was part of the Clint Brawner team. Number 12 saw a lot of action on the USAC Championship Trail at tracks like Milwaukee, Phoenix, and Trenton, New Jersey.

This car has an offset engine, but the engine sits upright and very low in the chassis. This is a refined four-bar suspension; Kuzma used split torsion bars front and rear that meet in the middle.

The car appears as it would have at Phoenix during the 1965 season.

This Eddie Kuzma version of the roadster was once driven by Mario Andretti. Number 12 saw a lot of action on the USAC Championship Trail at tracks like Milwaukee, Phoenix, and Trenton, New Jersey. Note the typical roadster details such as the chrome nerf bar in the rear, the distinctive grille-opening shape, and external, left-side oil tank alongside the engine. *Don Lyon Collection*

In the 1965 Indy 500, Bobby Unser wrecked his new four-wheel-drive Novi-Fergie in practice, but raced this 1964 car, qualifying eighth and finishing in 19th position. This is the last in a long line of famous, but heartbreaking, American race cars—the Novi Specials.
Motorsports Hall of Fame

REAR ENGINE REVOLUTION

1964/65 GRANATELLI STP NOVI

When Australian Jack Brabham chauffeured John Cooper's underpowered but nimble British Cooper-Climax to an easy ninth-place finish in the 1961 Indianapolis 500, it may not have been the handwriting on the wall, but it was certainly the graffiti. The other 32 cars were all front-engined roadsters from the shops of Watson, Epperly, Kuzma, Trevis, Lesovsky, and the father of the roadster, Frank Kurtis.

Brabham's little "funny car," as it was quickly nicknamed by the Indy folks, not only gave up 87 cubic inches and 140 horsepower to the roadsters, it was also 10-miles-per-hour slower down the straights. Its top speed was 150 miles per hour versus the roadsters' 160. Further, the car was hobbled by troublesome British Dunlop tires that wore more quickly than Firestones.

How did it manage to do so well? The Cooper weighed 400 pounds less and got better fuel economy (fewer pit stops) than the roadsters. The most profound difference was that it was 5 miles per hour faster through Indy's four corners. Brabham could drive flat out around the course at a steady 145 miles per hour.

Over the next ten years USAC Championship racing would see incredible changes in cars and technology. Rear-engined funny cars from the European Formula One scene unseated the traditional roadsters of the previous decade. Ford Motor Company officially returned to racing (on many fronts) and spent millions developing a new overhead-cam V-8. Goodyear threatened Firestone for dominance and instigated the tire wars. But a few ideas from earlier eras refused to lie down and die.

Always a sentimental favorite with racing fans, the Novi V-8s continued to soldier on under Andy Granatelli's ownership. Hopes were bright, but results were dim.

From his first appearance in the 1946 Classic with a refurbished Miller-Ford, the Grancor Special, Granatelli always stood a little to the left of the Indy establishment. A marketer, promoter, showman, innovator, and self-made millionaire, Andy was always looking for something different. His 1966 STP Lotus was the only car to ever run Indy with whitewall tires!

Always a sentimental favorite with racing fans, the Novi V-8s continued to soldier on under Andy Granatelli's ownership. Hopes were bright, but results were dim.

The idea of harnessing the Novi's incredible horsepower with the traction of four-wheel drive must have appealed to Andy, the ex-hot rodder.

Earlier Novis used Kurtis-Kraft front-drive chassis. This Ferguson four-wheel-drive chassis appeared in 1964 with Bobby Unser driving. Unser started 22nd, but was involved in the fiery first-lap Eddie Sachs-Dave McDonald crash. Malone started in 30th position in the old Kurtis-Kraft/Novi and managed to finish 11th.

In the 1965 Indy 500, Bobby Unser wrecked his new four-wheel-drive Novi-Fergie in practice, but raced this 1964 car, qualifying eighth and finishing in 19th position. Jim Hurtubise, in the old Kurtis-Kraft/Novi went out after one lap with transmission problems.

Although it had been tried many times, 1965 was the last attempt to utilize four-wheel drive on oval tracks. Rear-engine technology and wider tires with better traction finally put this idea to rest. This car is an authentic original.

1964 LOTUS-FORD

This Lotus Type 34 chassis with 255-ci Ford aluminum "Type-R" V-8 was driven by Jimmy Clark in the 1964 Indianapolis 500, under the Team Lotus, Ltd. banner. Although the Offenhauser engines produced 80 more horsepower than the Ford, the Lotus-Ford weighed only 1,150 pounds versus 1,600 pounds for the front-engined roadsters.

Clark won the pole with this car. His qualifying speed was 158.828 miles per hour. Clark led in the early laps of this race, but retired on lap 47 when one of his Dunlop tires began to shred and destroyed his rear suspension.

For the rest of the 1964 season Vels-Parnelli Jones Racing ran the car, with Parnelli Jones driving. He won in Milwaukee in August and in Trenton in September.

Had this car been running on different tires, it might have accomplished in 1964 what Jimmy Clark did one year later—an Indy 500 victory. *Parnelli Jones Collection*

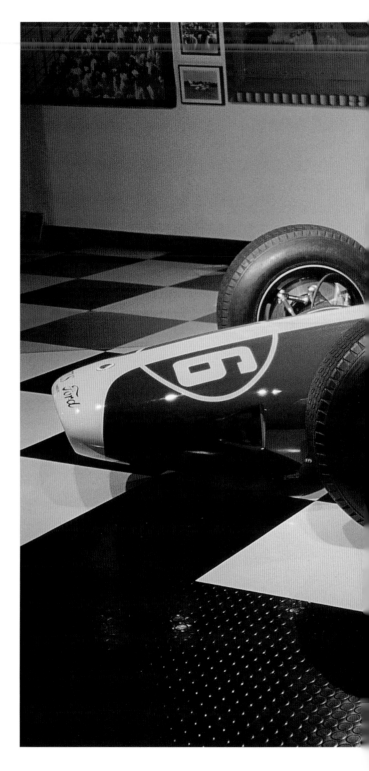

This car finally did it once and for all. The single most pivotal car in racing's modern era, this car won the Indy 500 in 1965 and forever sealed the fate of traditional front-engined cars in championship racing. *Ford Dearborn Museum*

Both tracks were paved. A.J. Foyt cleaned up the rest of the season's dirt-track races with his front-engined Watson roadster, the Sheraton-Thompson Special.

As built by Lotus Cars, Ltd. in England, the Type 34 was considered unsafe because it was too lightly built for American racing conditions. In fact, Lotus cars of this era had a nasty reputation for breaking with alarming frequency.

The Vels-Parnelli team extensively modified the car with help from Eddie Kuzma. New body panels were fitted to allow an increase in fuel capacity, and all suspension arms and links were changed to stronger tubing. The uprights and wheel hubs were changed to make the car safer and stronger, albeit heavier, under the direction of Johnny Paulsen, Jones' chief mechanic.

In 1967 at Langhorne, Pennsylvania, with Arnie Knepper driving, the car went airborne over another car. Although wrecked and burned, it was stored for a year, then brought back to the Vels-Parnelli shop in Torrance, California in 1968. In 1995 Phil Riley in San Francisco completed a ground-up restoration costing in excess of $100,000. Since then the car has been in the Parnelli Jones collection.

Jones drove this authentic, original car at the Monterey Historics in 1995.

1965 JIMMY CLARK LOTUS-FORD

The 1965 Indianapolis 500 was almost anti-climatic. Jimmy Clark qualified in second place behind A.J. Foyt. Then, on race day, Clark went out and won handily. Foyt fell out on lap 115 with gear trouble and finished 15th.

The story here is one of engines rather than chassis. Beginning in 1963, Ford Motor Company

Two NACA ducts on either side of the cockpit direct air into a large, white, fiberglass plenum. This plenum provides intake and cooling air for the turbine engine. *Parnelli Jones Collection*

threw its tremendous engineering and financial resources into the development of a radical new racing engine that would return them to the forefront of motor racing. They succeeded.

Clark's engine (and Foyt's) was a 255-ci, four-cylinder, overhead-cam V-8 unit. It was capable of putting out 450 dependable horsepower at a conservative 8,200 rpm.

For the next five years this was a favorite engine for Indy cars. It was challenged only by the venerable Offenhauser, now reduced to 168 cubic inches, but sporting powerful turbochargers that literally breathed new life into this aging four-cylinder engine.

Jack Brabham's 1961 introduction of light, maneuverable, rear-engined machines at Indy started a hard-fought, four-year technical revolution that culminated with this car's win in the 1965 Indy 500. This was a pivotal car for big-league Indy car racing because it finally sealed the fate of the traditional front-engined, rear-drive Offy-powered roadsters. This is an original, authentic car.

The roadsters faded quickly, but the Offenhauser four-bangers, with constant re-development, hung on for years to come.

PARNELLI JONES' 1968 GRANATELLI TURBINE

In 1967 Andy Granatelli frightened the establishment with his first four-wheel-drive gas-turbine car. Parnelli Jones, in the #40 STP car, started and finished Indy in sixth place.

Turbine-engined cars made their second and final appearance at Indianapolis in 1968. Some say they were too controversial for the Indy establishment, Others say they may have been too good and, at least for the fans, too quiet!

This is the car in which Joe Leonard nearly won the 500 and the same car in which Mario Andretti slammed both himself and Art Pol-

This wedge-shaped, Lotus-built chassis demonstrates early efforts at making the entire car work as an aerodynamic shape as it moves through the air. *Parnelli Jones Collection*

lard, in the other turbine car, into the turn 9 wall at Riverside.

Lotus built the chassis and body. The Ferguson Company engineered and built the four-wheel-drive system. The power is taken off the front end of a Pratt & Whitney helicopter turbine. Behind the driver's seat and roll bar, the engine's power is converted through a transfer case with a chain belt. Two drive shafts distributed the power to differentials at the front and rear axles.

The turbine provided no compression-braking, as in a piston engine, so massive inboard disc brakes all around had to work much harder on this car. This chassis also used upright, inboard-mounted coil-over spring/shock units, easily adjustable with a knurled knob at the bottom of each.

Weighing only 260 pounds, this Pratt & Whitney turbine developed a healthy 500 shaft-horsepower. *Parnelli Jones Collection*

Not quite as advanced as European design, this car still uses a variety of bolt-on wings and fins. *Parnelli Jones Collection*

According to Jim Dilamarter, who tends the Parnelli Jones flock of classic race cars, "Our turbine cars weren't really all that much faster than the conventional engines, however, they did have a lot of torque and the four-wheel-drive set-up could get all of that to the ground. Also, the cars were so tractive and so flexible the drivers could drive them anywhere on the track. They loved that."

Did racing politics drive the turbines off the track? Dilamarter explains that, "USAC legislated against four-wheel-drive automobiles not against turbines. However they so greatly reduced the size of the turbine's intake with each succeeding year, it effectively rendered them competitively underpowered."

USAC claimed the deciding factor was one of cost, not turbine technology. Four-wheel drive added $75,000 to $100,000 to the cost of an Indy car chassis, yet contributed little to overall speed or lap times. Piston-engine car owners lobbied strongly against four-wheel-drive chassis and USAC ruled in favor of the majority. Had they not, within one year millions of dollars worth of conventional race cars would have been little more than last year's junk.

To his credit, Granatelli didn't give up easily. He lobbied and protested too. Then he filed a court case against USAC and lost. For the 1969 season USAC further reduced the turbine's air inlet size to 12 square inches bringing power down to an uncompetitive 400 horsepower. That was the last straw and the last year for turbines at the Brickyard.

Firestone owned these cars along with STP and "gave" the car to Vels-Parnelli to campaign throughout the year, but the cars didn't do well on the shorter tracks in the USAC Championship series. This is an authentic, original car.

This "P. J. Colt" chassis won Indy in 1970 and 1971 driven by Al Unser Sr. *Parnelli Jones Collection*

1970 "JOHNNY LIGHTNING" P.J. COLT CHASSIS

The decade of the 1970s saw self-taught mechanics give way to technicians and university-educated engineers and designers. The wind tunnel joined the engine dynamometer as an important car-development tool. Turbocharging rather than supercharging was first used seriously and developed extensively during this period. And years of clumsy attempts at "streamlining" gave way to the arcane science of "aerodynamics."

American oval-track racing saw a resurgence of the internationalism originally envisioned by its founding fathers. New Zealander Bruce McClaren's cars designed by Gordon Coppuck were probably the fastest and most significant cars of this period.

The 159-ci, turbocharged Ford OHC V-8, developed in England was the dominant engine of this period, but the turbo-Offys filled half the starting positions in the 1970 Indianapolis 500 and the rest of the season.

This "P. J. Colt" chassis won Indy in 1970 driven by Al Unser Sr. Dilamarter explains, "It's a derivation of the Lola chassis, built from the ground up under the direction of Vels-Parnelli Racing's chief mechanic George Bignotti."

Jones' home-grown chassis is a "transitional" design that incorporated the best of recent developments and pointed the way to the future. This car used a monocoque "tub" chassis, but still used additional struts to support the engine and rear suspension. It flirted with aerodynamics, incorporating small winglets and side pods at the rear of the car. Front and rear wings would come next year. The engine had yet to become a stressed member of the overall chassis. Its sloping nose presented a low profile to the wind, but it was still the major air intake. Shovel noses and side pods would come later. This is an authentic original.

Front and rear tires have grown so wide they present their own problems because of aerodynamic drag. *Antique Auto and Race Car Museum*

WINGS AND FINS

Lap speeds or qualifying speeds don't tell the whole story of any particular racing series because in any one year changes to the rules or car specifications can drastically affect performance. However it is impossible to ignore the quantum gains during the end of the "vintage era."

The decade of the 1960s saw the mid-engine revolution. In 1960 Eddie Sachs, driving a front-engined roadster, took the Indy 500 pole with a qualifying speed of 146.592 mph. Ten years later Al Unser, Sr. took the 1970 pole at 170.221 mph with a mid-engined P. J. Colt chassis—a 23.63 mph jump.

The decade of the 1970s brought the innovation of aerodynamics. Al Unser, Sr.'s pole speed was eclipsed by Johnny Rutherford's 1980 mark of 192.526 mph—a 22.31 mph increase. A total increase of 45.93 mph in 20 years was more than any other period in Indy history.

However, by the early 1980s these years of rapid change had settled back to small, yearly refinements of the existing technologies—with one major difference.

By the 1983 season the 13-race Indy car schedule included not only paved superspeedway ovals, but five road courses.

Gone were the days of offset chassis and "left turn only" engineering. Road courses demanded cars that handled left and right and both sweeping and hairpin turns with equal grace. Engine, tire, and suspension improvements were important but weren't the complete answer. Cornering speed was the way to faster lap speeds. To increase cornering speed, the cars had to "stick" better through the turns. Management of the airflow over the car was the solution.

1983 MARCH-COSWORTH

The first rear-mounted "wings," actually upside-down airfoils that created negative pressure (downforce), first appeared in 1965 on Jim Hall's Chaparral 2C/2D. Mario Andretti's 1969 Indy winner had wings. Wings were also in use on midgets in 1970. By 1972 all Indy cars had sprouted them—front and rear. They worked very well. So well they soon grew to amazing proportions and lap speeds were edging into the danger zone. From 1971 to 1972 the pole speed at Indy jumped 18 miles per hour, an almost unbelievable advance. For the following seasons USAC instituted strict limitations on wing size and placement and designers began looking for other areas of race cars to improve.

In this composite-aluminum and carbon-fiber tub chassis, typical of the early 1980s, the driver sits far forward to make room for the fuel cell behind him. *Antique Auto and Race Car Museum*

Wind-tunnel testing showed that reshaping the car's undertray, especially the area between the cockpit and the side pods, created a negative pressure zone between the car and the pavement when traveling at speed. Since the air pressure under the car was less than the pressure of the air flowing over the body the car was being suctioned to the track surface. The faster the car went, the better it worked.

"Ground-effects" cars were first seen at Indy in 1979. The idea caught on quickly. By 1980, 30 percent of the starting grid used ground-effects designs.

The Bignotti-Cotter team fielded this car for the 1983 PPG-CART series with Kevin Cogan driving. In the early 1980s a March chassis with a Cosworth 161-ci, turbocharged V-8 engine was the way to go. Thirty-two Cosworths and one lone Chevy 355-ci stock-block started this race. This March-Cosworth started 22nd and finished fifth. Most of the chassis were Marches, with Penskes, Lola, and Eagles filling in the rest of the field.

The Bignotti-Cotter team were mid-field starters and finishers throughout the season, and the car's additional racing history is unknown. With top-flight teams demanding new equipment every year, it is safe to assume this car's racing career ended with the last race of the season at Phoenix International Raceway.

Under the auspices of the Ford Motor Company, development of the Ford-Cosworth four-cam V-8 began in 1965 in England, and over the next 10 years achieved great success in European Formula One racing. The engine came to Indy in the mid-1970s. Vels-Parnelli Jones Racing was the first team to experiment with this engine for use at Indianapolis. For the 1976 season they'd developed their own new Parnelli chassis around this engine.

It was a compact all-aluminum V-8, with double-overhead camshafts, four valves per cylinder, fuel injection, and turbocharging. It produced a reliable

The troublesome and always controversial turbocharger pop-off valve. *Antique Auto and Race Car Museum*

800 horsepower at 11,000 rpm, and by 1980 was the dominant engine in Indy car racing.

The Cosworth engine also facilitated a major breakthrough in chassis design that remains with us today—the use of the engine as a structural part of the car's chassis. The gearbox, rear suspension components, and rear wing were all bolted to the engine block. The engine was then bolted to a solid aluminum bulkhead immediately behind the fuel cell and driver's seat, where the chassis tub ends. The engine literally formed the back half of the car.

This original March-Cosworth, though 15 years old, represents modern race car development. Its basic design elements have been refined, but not drastically changed since 1983.

A composite carbon-fiber and aluminum monocoque tub, it is driven by a mid-engine, turbocharged V-8 that is a structural part of the chassis. The independent front and rear suspension is controlled by inboard-mounted, cockpit-adjustable, coil-over spring/shock units. Fifteen-inch tires in the rear and 10-inch front tires, vented hydraulic disc brakes, front and rear wings, and a ground-effects underbody combine to glue the car to the race track.

The curtain came down on the Offenhauser engine in 1983. Team owner Rolla Vollstedt arrived at Indy with the last Offy-engined racer. Driver Mark Alderson passed his rookie test in the car, but in a rain-shortened session Alderson didn't get to qualify. Surrounded by the high-tech scream of turbocharged V-8s, battered by motor racing's arcane politics and regulations, and bereft of further development time or money, the once-mighty Offenhauser engine passed quietly into racing history.

For the 1983 Indianapolis 500, Kevin Cogan qualified this car at 201.528 mph. Seventy two years earlier, on May 30, 1911, Ray Harroun wrestled and sweated with his ill-handling, oil-spewing Marmon Wasp at a race-winning 74.602 mph.

In 1911 the average Indy competitor was lucky to squeeze 100 horsepower from a 500-ci engine. By 1983 engines produced eight times that horsepower from 161 cubic inches.

In 1983 drivers talked in terms of g-force, down force, slip angles, bump steer, ride height, turbo boost, and lift/drag coefficient. In 1911 drivers talked about just hanging on for 500 miles.

You could describe 1911 race cars as just slightly more automobile than buckboard. By 1983 drivers progressed to cars that were just slightly more automobile than airplane.

BIBLIOGRAPHY

Bochroch, Albert R. *American Automobile Racing*. New York, NY: Viking Press, 1974.

Brown, Allan E. *The History of America's Speedways*. Comstock Park, MI: self-published 1994.

Devaney, John & Barbara. *The Indianapolis 500*. Chicago: Rand McNally, 1976.

Fox, Charles. *The Great Racing Cars and Drivers*. New York, NY: Grossett & Dunlap, 1972.

Fox, Jack C. *The Illustrated History of the Indianapolis 500*. Speedway, IN: Carl Hungness, 1984.

Fox, Jack C. *The Illustrated History of Sprint Car Racing*, volume 1. Speedway, IN: Carl Hungness, 1985.

Hungness, Carl. *USAC Sprint History 1956–1980*. Speedway, IN: Carl Hungness, 1994.

Huntington, Roger. *Design & Development of the Indy Car*. Tucson, AZ: HP Books, 1981.

Pritchard, Anthony. *Maserati: A History*. New York, NY: Arco, 1976.

Rendall, Ivan. *The Checkered Flag*. Secaucus, NJ: Chartwell, 1993.

Sakkis, Tony. *Anatomy & Development of the Indy Car*. Osceola, WI: Motorbooks International, 1994.

Sawyer, John. *The Dusty Heroes*. Speedway, IN: Carl Hungness, 1994.

Taylor, Rich. *INDY: Seventy-five Years*. New York, NY: St. Martin's Press, 1991.

White, Gordon Eliot. *Offenhauser*. Osceola, WI: Motorbooks International, 1996.

INDEX